# HOW A CHRISTIAN CAN FALL

from

EZEKIEL OPE ALEX

# HOW A CHRISTIAN CAN FALL FROM GRACE TO GRASS



First Edition
ISBN:978-978-991-061-8
Unless otherwise indicated, scripture quotations are from the King James Version of the Holy Bible.

Published in Nigeria by;
New Light Publications
1, Onafuwa Street, Ogba-Ashade, Agege, Lagos, Nigeria.
Tel.: 2348102148389; 2348094755642.
Email: newlight4ng@yahoo.com

# FORWARD

When the manuscripts of **"HOW A CHRISTIAN CAN FALL FROM GRACE TO GRASS"** was given to me to proof-read and subsequently write the forward, I was convinced immediately that it was what I want to do,even before I opened the scripts.

The Writer, Brother Ezekiel Alex has really put on a light necessary for a Christian to walk via the rugged route of faith to overcome the fiery darts of Satan that often entangle an unwary Christian to backslide, and possibly give-up the faith if not checked.

Initially, I thought the scripts were for tracts but, with the book in my hands now, the depth of insight and readability of the contents conquered my own expectations. As a matter of need, I am poised to recommend and urge every Christian to own a copy of this book; and give it as gift to fellow Christians, new converts in the Churches, at Revival programmes and Crusades.

I recommend that Ministers, Evangelists, Missionaries and Church Planters will get hold of this book and urge new converts who turn to Christ through their Ministries to have it that they may learn to avoid those ways of Satan's tricks which he displays to draw them down from grace to grass. God forbid! Christians in general are meant to remain victorious in the battle of faith by Jesus Christ to grow into spiritual maturity with such revelations contained in this book.

Brother Ezekiel is a young Christian-soul-winner, who has known the troubles and trials new converts, and some matured Christians encounter in the midst of the evils around us. Get it! Read it!! And practice it!!! I prophesy that this book will make out something spiritually positive and new in your life; and you will never go back to square one, in Jesus' name, amen.

**Rev. Dr. Wisdom Mbanali**

# ACKNOWLEDGMENT

I am grateful to God for His Grace upon my life through Christ Jesus for this Book. By the Grace of God, I want to acknowledge the following people for their support that made this Publication a reality: Pastor Moses Lawal, Regional Overseer of Mountain of Fire And Miracles Ministries; Miss P.S. Moses for her financial support; Precious, Alex (Families) and Mr.Wole, my In-Law for their morals.

Brother, Joshua Duru for his Kind gesture and courage. I also want to thank the Church and Sanctuary Keepers/Technical Crew Groups of Mountain Of Fire And Miracles Ministries for their prayers; and my alltime caring Pastors for their spiritual guidance through the years.

# DEDICATION

This book is written by me but the knowledge comes from God; everyone who read this book shall be blessed by the power of our Lord Jesus Christ.

# Contents: PAGE:

# INTRODUCTION

***How a Christian can fall from Grace to grass'*** simply talks about how Christians practice ungodly and worldly acts such as sin, whether secretly, openly or otherwise, it will be revealed.

Those who call themselves Christians but inwardly they are far from God and also love their comfortable zone: while they think they are prospering but they are not; and if they are not careful, they may not rise again and finally affect their children with it. This is why Lord Jesus said *"strive"* but do not be too comfortable with the situation you find yourself lest it destroys you; your comfort zone is Heaven.

It also means skeleton one has in his/her cupboard. The way that take them back to square one is their ignorance to God and obedience to the world and the things thereof. It also means one can be an Ichabod - meaning the glory of God has departed; the one that is most painful is what the Lord Jesus said *"when men slept his enemy came and sow tares in his life"*(). This is what drags many people back to square one because through it the wiles of devil will work well.

# #1:MONETARY SPIRIT:

This is the love of money, material things and lust for it; it is also called mammon. It is not bad to have money or to work for it legally but very bad to love it more than God or use it for evil purposes like using it to lead others astray, rituals, stealing, killing and fraudulent acts. Even the Lord Jesus said

> *"No man can serve two masters: for either he will hate the one, and love the other; or else he will hold to the one, and despise the other. Ye cannot serve God and mammon* (Matthew 6:24);

But there is a way that seem right and the end is destruction. Money answers all things but wisdom overrules it and to have wisdom, one must have the fear of God. Many are hopping from bed to bed because of money; many are stealing more than their wages: using their wages to enrich themselves and also careless about what they are doing because they believe if the poor and needy refuse to work there are one thousand and one or more people to replace them with: And through this act many have engaged in ungodly acts that is uncalled for and they use it to oppress the poor. Many will leave God out of the picture of their lives and also commit crimes that's why the word of God instruct that one has to be contented with his/her wages and not covet others' wages.

Many are so desperate to acquire wealth because they say they do not want to be left behind amongst their equals: And by this reasoning alone, they give themselves to fetish things to acquire wealth and that makes them God's enemy. It just like the one I knew that coached a team of footballers but he was not contented with what he was getting, though God prospered him there but he was so desperate to make quick money and own properties, it is more like a person running faster than his/her shadow.

He deceived his players and they were bringing money to him because he promised them visa and also play football overseas but unfortunately, the thing backfired on him and he was arrested by the force. Quick success that is not of God is not welcome by God because it is evil and brings doom to one's life and also makes God go farther from one. God promised Joseph to be someone special through dreams: And thank God for his father, Jacob that led him to God because he set example for his children to follow, which they did but Joseph was more preferable than his brethren for two reasons which are obedience and a son of his old age.

Despite all his brethren did to him because he told them of his dreams: They were envious of him and hated him; they planned to kill him; but later him sold into slavery so that the dream would not manifest. The eldest son of Jacob stopped them from killing him, hence they threw him into the well, after a while they brought him out and sold him to slavery but he never left God and, God favored him in the land of bondage, Egypt. His master Potiphar knew that God blessed him because of Joseph and he made him overseer of his properties except his wife. Although the wife of his master was lustful of him but he never agreed and she grabbed his garment he was wearing and used it to frame him up. He was thrown into prison, still he did not give up on God and he was favored in the prison and there he met the servants of Pharaoh. They had dreams but no one could explain it to them and they were terrified by it, then Joseph knew that the countenance of their faces was not right with them. He asked them what was the problem and, they asked him if he can interpret dreams: He exalted God because he knew that God can do all things and there is nothing hard for Him to do.

He said to them interpretation belongs to God and they told him their dreams and he explained it by the spirit of God upon him. They were pleased because he interpreted it well and he asked one of them to remember him when he is restored back to his position, but he never remembered Joseph until Pharaoh had terrible dreams. He called for all his sorcerers and magicians but none of them could interpret the dream to him, then one of Pharaoh's servants remembered that the Lord had used Joseph to interpret his dream and he told Pharaoh about Joseph. Pharaoh sent for Joseph and told him, his dreams and to the glory of God, he interpreted the meaning of the dreams to him and that was how God used Pharaoh to make Joseph second in command over Egypt; he became more superior over his former master, Potiphar.

Everything in life follows some process; and one has to go through it to become wise, strong, teachable, resourceful and accomplished in life. However, people are fond of saying some are born with golden spoon and silver spoon but they have eyes and see not; they have ears and hear not.

The truth most people do not know is this; God cannot be bewitched in His image: He made you and I, including those that we claim to be born with golden and silver spoons; we are the image of God but the sin of Adam and Eve made things awful and the devil can be called all sorts of names; but never call him a fool because he knew what he wanted by telling Adam and Eve to eat from the forbidden fruit called *"the tree of knowledge of good and evil"*(Genesis 2:17), but the devil never told Eve to eat from the Tree of Life which is the Word of God and Life in Abundance.

Many parents will regret it if they fail to train their children in the ways of the Lord and, they may eventually end up like Eli because he did not give his children good upbringing: Also Eli lack the fear of God and that brought big disgrace to him, for he was cursed by God and his children were killed by the sword of their enemies and he died when he got the news. For the word of God says,

> *"if the foundation be destroyed what can the righteous do?"*(Psalm 11:3).

This is a question asked but none could answer until Lord Jesus came and gave the answer to it because He said,

> *"Anyone that hears the saying of his, he will like him to be a wise man, for a man that build his house on sand and the rain cometh and the house shaketh then such man is a fool but he that build his house on the rock, the rain cometh and the house shaketh not then he is a wise man"* (Matthew 7:24-26).

What He is talking about is our foundation and a wise person will make with Him, his/her strong tower because He is the Rock of our Salvation, without Him we can do nothing, and there is no dominion with anybody but Jesus Christ because He has overcome the wiles of the devil and his cohorts, and the world as well; all power and authority has been given to Him by the Father, God almighty. Those who allow money to have control over them are not fortunate but have been subdued by the power of mammon spirit. Some are saying if we do not have money what are we living for, it is because they are not thankful nor see what God has been doing for them since they were born. Some are ashamed of coming to the house of God: they do not want people to mock them or laugh at them because they are not rich, even clothes they do not have, even tithe and offering they hardly give: but the truth is that you give your heart and life to God to govern as your Lord and Savior, and make your service a living sacrifice and an offering to God. Come to church and do not be ashamed but be not contented with it, give yourself fully for God to use, pray and fast, let your children have the fear of God in you, do not give up on God because He has broken yokes, bondages, afflictions and wiles of the devil for your sake. He loves you and you must be thankful for the life He has given you.

Many are in the hospitals, cemetery, mortuary, but God kept you alive to be in His Sanctuary that is more than enough to be thankful for and He deserves all the glory. Those who put their trust in riches shall fall because money or wealth, cars, fame, even the earth is temporary and not permanent, only God is Everlasting to Everlasting. There are things that money can buy and cannot buy at the same time which are sleep, death, life, air, salvation, prayer, fasting, holiness, righteousness, godliness, appetite, happiness, sadness, sorrow, joy, love, hate, redemption, eternity, wisdom, knowledge and understanding, etc.

# #2: CULTISM

This is a satanic or demonic domain. 'Cultism' has never helped, promoted or done any good to the society. It causes catastrophe and woes, makes one rude and disobedient because of the dark power one believes in and it profits one nothing. There is a Great power (the Power of God) that has done well to humans but many have forsaken it because they love darkness. How would they not love darkness when their father, Satan made Adam and Eve to eat from the *"tree of the knowledge of good and evil"* because he wants to rule but, God cast him away out of heaven?

Thank God for the Bible and the words in it because there is a way that seems right unto a man but the end thereof is the way of destruction; those trending on this path will surely regret it because they have wasted their time, and time wasted cannot be recovered because the time that was supposed to be used for something resourceful that God has ordained for you but, the same devil that misled Adam and Eve is already misleading you. The devil loves no one but himself and he knows that destruction awaits him and his cohorts. The Lord knew what he is from the beginning that he is full of evil and subtle in nature: Even when the Lord Jesus started His work and was casting out demons, some of the demons were spoke through their possessed saying,

> *"what have I to do with thee, Jesus, thou Son of the most high God? I adjure thee by God, that thou torment me not."*(Mark 5:7).

For a man possessed by demons to say this then even humans should sit up because the Great day of the Lord is at hand. There was a time a young man joined a cult because he wanted the power and respect. He did not really focus on his education. He was a school dropout, he goes to people's shops and homes to ask for money and if they delay to give to him on time, he takes whatever he wants and takes it home to his mother, but she never rebuked him and he was doing that over and over again.

Until one day, he was with his groups collecting money from a man that was just repairing the front of the entrance of his house which had been there for years but they said 'they will collect money from him, that it does not concern them because that is how they get their money, and it is the instruction they follow'; the man gave them money and, after a while again the young man that joined cult came back and requested for money and the old man said to him, 'my son if I continue to give out the money you are asking for what would I use to finish the work and beside this house has been here for years' but this young man was wroth with the old man and slapped him for saying that to him because he believes that whatever he asks for, he must get it; then the old man called him back and said to him "I know you very well, even your father is an old man but I am older than him and I know that you have been warned but here is the truth as the spirit of the lord leads me will I say to you, you have just seven days in life" but he never listened and proudly walked away from the old man. He believed in the power of darkness he relies upon which is the cult he belongs to and unfortunately for him, he fell into a big trouble that the demon that was pushing him left him and he was killed by the law enforcement agency.

There are some that show the signs and logo of their cult even in Christianity, they show you two fingers in the air and say it is called "peace" when there is no peace with them. The devil dwells in them and they are his servants. The Bible says,

> *"Ye are of your father the devil, and the lusts of your father ye will do. He was a murderer from the beginning, and abode not in the truth, because there is no truth in him. When he speaketh a liar, he speaketh of his own: for he is a liar and the father of it"*(John 8:44). And the Lord Jesus says, *"The thief cometh not, but for to steal, and to kill, and to destroy: I am come that they might have life, and that they might have it more abundantly"* (John 10:10).

The devil has come to steal, kill and destroy. Lord Jesus said on the Cross of Calvary *"Father forgive them; for they know not what they do"*(Luke 23:34). They think they know when the prince of this world resides in them and his major assignment is to seek their destruction. The language they use is uncalled for and all of them are demonic; some jam their hands against each other like an Axe, some walk in group and welcome each other with a language they organized for themselves.

In politics, when it is not yet time for election, you hardly hear of blood shed but when it comes up, they use people against one another while they are using that to enrich themselves in evil. Some will promise you things like good roads, stable light, good schools with qualified teachers and so on but never would tell you of Jesus because they cannot give you what they do not have, that is Jesus. Without Jesus there is nothing one can offer you because they will eventually hurt you one way or the other. Prophet Samuel told the children of Israel not to seek for human king but God, that have been with them on their journey to the promised land but they were strong headed even when he told them of what will befall them but they did not hear and now they are complaining because they have seen the repercussion of what they asked for.

There is cultism everywhere in the society because according to them for one to excel in life one has to be fortified and be in their amongst them or you will be wasted by the enemy which dwells in them but they have not the knowledge of God and the book of Hosea tells us, *"my people are destroyed for lack of knowledge"* (Hosea 4:6). What you don't know have power over you. Cultism is everywhere like I said before and they are seen in Music Industry, Movie Industry, Politics, Jobs, Churches because all that glitters are not gold; almost everything in the society belong to one cult or the other. If you think that joining a cult to prosper your children or to enrich yourself is alright for you, then you do not know why you are alive because even economics says human wants are unlimited. God used Moses, His servant to lead about three million souls out of Egypt, yet they were not contented with what God gave to them.

They were told of what will befall them if they hearken to other gods to serve them but still they went back to their old ways because they are slaves to their yokes and forty days journey became forty years. Whatever evil you have done is to make your burden and that of your children dark, and yokes shall be hard for you to bear, and through this the devil will have power to torment you and your seeds. The devil cannot tell you the complete truth; and half-truth is no truth but complete lies and the wiles of the devil will be played very well on you and your household; that's why you see some families that are doing well before and all of a sudden things become hard for them and they are also known to be Ichabod. If the foundation be destroyed what can the righteous do? I can remember what a man told me some years back, when I worked for a company that sells home appliances, he said to me, the company you are working for won't pay you beside there are other things you can do which I am also enjoying.

I looked around his shop, he sells movies / music in compact discs; and he said I should not look at that because this one I see here are camouflage; he asked if I am a Christian, I told him nothing but the truth that I am. Later, he said that won't stop him from saying what he has to tell me because many call themselves Christian but they are not even close to the word ***Christian*** neither do they have Christ-like nature in them. He said if I can get Five Thousand Naira, he will tell me what to do and I should be close to where fire is like candle or lamp and say some words which he won't tell me except I am ready to do what he said but there is something he knows which is, that the money will be placed on top of the fire and it won't burn but be taken by the fire to appear somewhere else and the people in charge of it will know who sent it to them and also put a book in the fire and it will appear to me and I should read it and I will have power and wealth. The name of the book is ***Seven Books of Moses.*** Truly, I was shocked to hear the word Seven Books of Moses because I know that the spirit of the Lord made him write these books "Genesis, Exodus, Leviticus, Numbers and Deuteronomy": And how come he wrote seven when the true one says he only wrote five books of the Bible; but by then I knew that he was not happy, and he said I should not misquote the Bible for him and besides there are many people he knows where I live that are using the book to empower themselves and also have wealth. I was shocked when he mentioned someone that I know but he said he does not have to practice it but he is good at his hand work as an electrician. Wake up children of God, put on the whole Armor of God to stand against the wiles of the devil. To be able to withstand it, one has to have all the attributes of Godliness inside and outside, not pretending; but completely giving your life to Christ in truth and in spirit.

Like I said earlier; there are cultists everywhere now, like in Music, Movies, Churches (For the Bible says; many are called but few are chosen), Schools, even at Work places; and most of the shows we watch on television. How can someone want to sleep with you because he promised to get you a job but; or they may get you a job and ask you to do whatever it takes to bring in money because they have given you target of such amount that even themselves cannot get, but still make you believe you can make it happen because according to them, you use what you have to get what you want in life.

In music, the words they use which seem to glorify God but speak demonic incantations they call slang; and if you do not have God in truth and spirit you will fall victim to their trap. Sometime past I heard that some of the beats they use are not ordinary because it means something evil and could make someone spend unnecessarily and later regrets it. Some of the shows we watch are wiles of the devil to get you into their trap because it is neither teaching any moral nor reflect Godliness. They gather many people in a place and tell them to do whatever they ask them to do and if anyone refuses, such will be disqualified whether it be moral or immoral, it does not matter, whether it adds value to one's life or decreases you spiritually because many do not know that the spiritual controls the physical In the movies, we hear words that are not suitable for people under eighteen years of age; then you wonder what that will teach you that is above eighteen years because it may still not be appropriate for you to watch: Is it the immoral part, the fighting, the lying, the romance, and so on – these are corruptible displays and make one imagine them to corrupt one's mind. The church part is the most painful one, you are called for divine purpose not for selfish reasons; you are the children of the light, let it shine by reflecting Christ Jesus in all you do and say; you call yourself a Christian, yet you don't have love but hate, you love to fight and quarrel with anybody and you use words like;

> *'that Jesus was righteous in all that he did while on earth does not mean I will be like him; but, because I know God to be merciful I will deal with you and after dealing with you, I will go back to Him and ask for forgiveness; and I know He will forgive me'.*

That is why you steal from the church, you gossip here and there just to lead people astray or you are one leg in the house of God and another outside His house but in the domain of witches and wizards; yet you are more like a blood sucking demon, or you are the type that teaches your members to worship a statue which cannot speak or frames of someone you want them to believe is Lord Jesus. But He is not the image because He said no one should worship any graven image or idol for He is a jealous God. They are the works of man's hand; and those who make them are just like them.

# #3: UNFORGIVING SPIRIT:

This is a spirit that hates to reconcile with someone that offends him / her especially when the person he/she hates is prospering. He / She hates the person more because such a person that is filled with the spirit of unforgiving will always blame others for their misfortune.A person with unforgiving spirit hinders his/her own blessing because the Lord forgives us our trespasses as we forgive those who trespass against us and He delivers us from trials, temptation and evil.
The Lord Jesus said *"Father, forgive them; for they know not what they do, ...* **(Luke 23:34):** To forgive heals you internally - yokes and burden will be lifted off you and you shall be one with the Lord because He abides in you and you in Him, just as He said *"For my yoke is easy, and my burden is light"* (Matthew 11:30).

Learn to forgive and to rebuke devourers; never allow the devil to be a member of the family or your home and also do not allow him to dwell in you. The devil is an enemy of progress; he has it in him and he is busy hating everyone that serves God in truth and spirit even when they did not offend him. Therefore, you that worship the Almighty God must walk with Him with all diligence and never go back to the world and its carnal ways that are unfruitful.

Unforgiving Spirit hinders prayers because the prayer of such that does not forgive is an abomination to the Lord as He does not have respect for such prayers: But it backfires at the person that offers the prayer with such act and spirit in him/her. It also hinders breakthroughs and places one in abject poverty and if time is not taken the seeds it brings out from you will not get helpers; but you will be running helter-skelter, going from place to place for solution yet not getting answer for solution: Yet when that are told to go and reconcile with those they are quarreling with, they refuse and the devil continues to play his wiles over them and if time is not taken properly, it will destroy because it is an addiction that has arrests the heart, so it is better to destroy it before it destroys you.

There is no sin that is too big to be forgiven: When we consider what the wicked and evil ones did to the Lord Jesus, yet He forgave them because He loves and gives grace for repentance, else one be consumed by it. Like I said before there is no sin that is too big to be forgiven: like unfaithfulness in marriage, stealing, killing, corruption, fornication and adultery, flattering, and so on. If Hosea can forgive his wife (Gomer) because she was unfaithful to him; when he sought for God's counsel, God told him that it is the same way the children of Israel rejected Him so had his wife rejected him. Yet, that did not make God to hate them neither did He fail to forgive them.

God is love, although He is patient but does not welcome sin. The mistakes Saul, the son of Kish made opened way for God to choose David to be king in Israel. If you are ready to remain not married nor bear with your wife/husband, then do not go into marriage because if you find your husband/wife cheating, you are meant to forgive him/her because it is your cross to bear. God is against divorce because it is the work of the devil and those that engage in it are also in accord with the works of the devil because how can you divorce one and go after another and you still say, 'he/she was a brute and doesn't know how to treat someone well' and that is why you left him/her for another; finally you find someone you feel is capable, beloved you are wrong because there is nothing prayer, fasting and fruits of the Spirit cannot solve by God's grace and power. Going from one man/woman to another is ***'adultery'*** and it is unfaithfulness in ***'marriage'***. Marriage is more than the ring you put on your finger; it is the vow of marriage that matters a lot. Unforgiving Spirit breeds hatred and bitterness and it does not bring solution to anyone neither does it shed light to dark moments; and above all it makes everyone your enemy: It even makes one an enemy of God because it is a reflection of the devil and his acts.

Some people are full of hatred for the evil done to them because when they were in position to help people they never helped: They never believed it is good to show kindness or be generous to other people, but when other people repay them with evil because things are not going well as expected; they see such ones and others they helped to be the devil that is after them. I once overheard one say, 'In this life one cannot be rich or doing well forever because a certain time will come when one will eventually fall back to square one'. This is the wiles of the devil that is been played on humans because the word of God says, *"The blessing of the lord, it maketh rich, and addeth no sorrow with it"* (Proverbs 10:22). Jabez was honorable amongst his brethren but he wasn't blessed because his mother also confessed to it and also said *"Jabez was born in sorrow"* but he cried unto the Lord and his reproach was taken off him and his life was transformed to the glory of God.

It is not the will of God for Job to be poor but the devil's because he is enemy of progress and good things: But Job never give up on God and the Lord used Elihu, the youngest amongst his three friends that visited him to revive him and God intervened in his situation - his life changed forever and he lived to see four generations of his time and God restored all that he lost back to him more than he ever had.

# #4: UNFAITHFUL SPIRIT

This is a spirit filled with lies and unbelief. Unfaithfulness produces infidelity, stealing, killing and unrighteous ego to be respected by people and also fill on top of the world. Unfaithfulness is seen in marriages: When you are married you must be faithful to one another, and if one commits sin or is seen having extra-marital affair with another person whether it be the woman/man should not be an excuse for the offended couple to repay evil for evil because only a fool will do that and the unfaithfulness has nothing to profit either of the couples in Christ. When Christ profits you more than every other thing; then you have no need to cheat or jilt one another in your marriage in obedience to the sacrament of marriage:

> *'For better for worse, for richer and for poorer, in sickness and in health, till death do us part'.* It is a vow not just ordinary agreement and the one that joined both of you is God and He is the Author of marriage (see, Genesis 2:21-25).

I learnt some definition of marriage in most gospel messages I listened to, and Christian movies I watched, which says:

> *'Marriage is like a Triangle, the man on the left, the wife on the right, and God is at the top of it; which means whatsoever God has joined together let no man, woman, lawyer, judge, legislator, judiciary, executive and pastors put asunder'.*

It also means that couples should look unto God the Author and Finisher of their faith: And without Him, they can do nothing because He is All in All. Every marriage must be built in Him, the only true Vine as explained in the Bible book of John, Chapter 15. He abides in you and you in Him and that is, a solid foundation in Christ Jesus.

You call yourselves servants of God and you still charge people money for your work of ministry just like the children of Eli did and they perished; or you lack the knowledge of God because you don't meditate upon the word of God and that can lead to destruction because many perish for lack of knowledge: You may say it is not common because old things are passed away and every other thing has become new then you are mistaking and finished.

Hebrews 13:8, tells us that God is the same yesterday, today and forever, which means God has not changed and He is called the '***Unchangeable Changer***'; so don't be deceived by your lust and selfish desires. Be contented with what you have; not being covetous or greedy because it has produced various disaster like kidnapping, stealing, ritual killing, internet frauds and so on because they did not wait on God but have given themselves to lust and deceit. You call yourself a true Christian but you don't obey the law of God nor walk according to His instructions embedded in His word. Many people are fond of saying,

> *'Don't judge me, if you don't want God to judge you'* or they use these words *'Jesus turned water into wine';*

so that becomes an access for you to drink and involved in various delinquent behaviours because you are spiritually porous; even you dress indecently and when you are corrected you say, *'God is not looking at the dressing but the heart'*; but mind you, what you don't know have power over you and it might destroy you because the same word of God says,

> *'ye that is guilty of one is guilty of all'.*

If your appearance does not reflect Christ then your heart is not right with Him but full of sin and it leads you to hell because what you are showing is called ***'self-righteousness'*:** The word of God says,

> *"There is a way that seem right unto a man but the end thereof is the way of death"* (Proverbs 14:12; 16:25).

Wake up from your slumber, and put on the Armor of God to stand against the wiles of the devil. You servant of God that invites comedians to your church to perform comedy, you are in all unfaithful and you need to rededicate your life to God so that your sin will not overtake and destroy you; for the wages of sin is death and you the comedian, that is coming to church to perform, continue because the word of God says *"Hold steadfast of what is with you for I come very soon to reward every man according to the works of his hands"* (Revelations 22:12).

The lord that rebuked those that wanted to turn the House of God into a house of merchandise and a den of thieves knows why He did that and now many want to turn His House of Prayer into a house of jesters where comedy is displayed to entertain people instead of salvation massage and prayer. There was a day, a man was preaching in my street and after a while he said, *'The lord has sent me here to kill you, including the rich ones that are not close to God neither do they have the fear of God';* then I noticed that after he said that he spoke demonic tongues and even warned the commercial motorcycle riders around using their motorcycle to make money and fend for themselves that they should go and read their Bibles or else he will slap them. After a while I noticed that most of the rich men were scared of him and his preaching. They confronted him and he told them that if they don't stay far away from him, he will slap them and they shall die because they don't know him and the power of God upon him. The truth is that the spirit that possesses the man is not of God but a contrary spirit of the devil and the devil knows the Bible because he preached and quoted the Bible to the Lord Jesus but the Lord overcame him.

The rich men were very much scared and terrified because of the way the man talks and they had no other choice but to involve the police, unknown to them that the man was not scared of the police they called, neither does he have any power to do them anything; yet they were so scared of him: These men boast to be Christians but love the things they possess according to the flesh and not the profitable things of the Spirit of God that leads to life eternal. Unfaithful Spirit is more like lust and its root is not good but bad, its end is always disastrous, it makes you to go astray and still make you believe God is just and merciful to forgive you, while you knowingly commit the sin. If you don't take time, it will eat you up like termites eat up a good wood but still make it look like a good one to the eyes: But it shatters when one sits on it because inside the wood has been eaten up by termites. You call yourselves Christians yet know how to deceive women into unrighteous living; or even covet after your neighbor's wife: But thus says the Lord;*"woe unto you or woe betides you!"* All the prostitutes know you and because you are their regular customer; you call yourself Christians, you know how to lie and hardly have time for God neither do you meditate in His word but still you claim to be a child of God and still tell people, it is not by fasting or prayer, but go to wherever you want because God is everywhere and catch your fun and enjoy it to the fullest.

You call yourself Christian but misled others to Hell because you are void of the knowledge of God neither do you obey His word in truth and spirit. You tell your members not to be bothered because Lord Jesus has paid the price for us all, there is no need to pray and fast nor seek for the Holy Spirit because He is in you and begin to shine for the master, flow in the Holy Ghost and see great signs and wonders that shall follow thee.

You tell them to serve God with swags when it is not heard not talk in the Bible, you give them motivational messages when you are supposed to preach salvation and heal the broken hearted, pray for the captives to be set free but no, you choose to go after your own lust. You cannot be a faithful Christian when you still live in lies; you lie to get things from people, you cheat people out of their property with lies, you bear false witness against your neighbor, you lie because someone didn't reciprocate the same feeling you have or had for him or her; and what most Christians do not know is that when one is unfaithful it chases helpers and no one will know whether you are doing well or not because there is a deception or deceit that lies within you.

The same spirit possesses the Devil, who was once called Lucifer as an Angel of the Lord but the Lord knew what he would become and He wrote His word in his heart and really he did because there is no truth in him while the one and only true God made him; but he choose to be a liar and also want God's throne because a liar is never satisfied nor contented with what he has but always choosing to get involved in any negative activity as a means of livelihood.

# #5: LIAR

This is a being with froward mouth - a mouth that says many words but none has been accomplished. A liar can never control himself/herself from lying to people and it's like the words of his/her mouth cannot be controlled by him/her and when it cannot be controlled by him/her, then it is very possible to over step your boundary because of the words of your mouth. Genesis 3:1-5 tells us how Adam and Eve were tempted by the devil and eventually they fall victims of his lies because he is the master of deception and there is neither truth nor good in him. He deceived them to eat from the *"tree of knowledge of good and evil"* because he is evil and wants to rule. On the other hand, the word of God tells us about God and it is not when He begins to talk and talk we can understand Him; meditate in His word because His word is Life.

The *"tree of knowledge of good and evil"* tells that God also made good and evil and He didn't hide it but God is good and not evil and at the same time ***'God is over principalities'*** so, if you don't want Him to be a Principality in your life, obey His word, commandment and statute and you will be free; even the devil will flee from you. As I was saying of the book of Genesis, Adam and Eve sinned against God when they ate from the fruit, He asked them not to eat and when God came down to them, they hid themselves from God and told Him that the serpent beguiled them to eat from the fruit He asked them not to eat. God cursed the serpent and then asked why they went ahead to eat of the fruits, but the words of Adam were so bad and wrong, which is; *"The woman you gave me, made me to eat of the forbidden fruit":*They were sent out of the Garden of Eden to where they will till the ground to get food and labor for it all the days of their lives; and the Garden of Eden is more like Paradise on Earth but lies and temptation made them lose it. A lying spirit will make you deaf and blind to the truth while you have eyes and ears to see and hear but because of what you put your trust it makes you not to obey nor hearken to it. There are many that put their trust in the material things they have acquired, some the fame to please people or the public, and they are also seen as public figure and; their life will be determined by the public because they are the ones that makes them get funds to live – so that makes them to forget God, their Creator. In Politics as well, they come out and give lies to people for their selfish interest and change when they have got the position they want and use it to maltreat the poor.

They take more than their wages and never care of the truth, which is sin and the wages of sin as the Bible tell us: *"the wages of sin is death"* (Romans 6:23). Many are dead spiritually while they are still alive; and it is through love of money, prostitution, fornication, adultery, lies, pornography, illicit relationship, negative words, rape, fraud, lust, unforgiving spirit, malice, hatred, backbiting and above all unbelief. Half-truth is no truth but lies; and gossip is also part of it, if it is not stopped, it will lead to one's destruction and it leads to hell because there are no big lies or small lies, for sin is sin and it leads to death. Liars in marriage will not prosper! The words you speak, which you think does not matter or that it will not affect you neither cause you any problem will definitely happen to you like you are caught in an ungodly act, but you know how to lie and you try to defend yourself by lying more, then be prepared for the consequences because what you don't know have power over you and you have sought for your own destruction. To the false pastor, prophet, prophetess, evangelist, apostle, politician, lecturer, professor, bishop, teacher, worker, thug, and so on; there is a way that seem right but the end is death because it is not ordained by God but lust, which is a branch from sin.

There is one I know that cannot do without lying, anything one says happened to him, she will say it has happened to her as well and helpers never came her way and through that act of lying she has given birth to many children because the master of deception pushes her into illicit relationships where men use sugar-coated words for her, which is still lies to sleep or make out with her. I can still remember when I was a teenager; there was a lady that lives in the same compound with me. Men usually come around to visit her, and most of them do not greet because they are full of pride and she laughs with their flattering words. There was a day, a handsome and young guy came to look for her and he greeted me and others around, despite we were teenagers and we were amazed by that because we have never seen such before and he was very humble, but unfortunately she refused him, she said he is too gentle for her liking and she cannot accept him; then she followed one that flatters her with words and when they were together, the one that flatters her with words beat her like they are in a boxing match. No one told her to run for her life but she talked to herself because she knew if it continues it will lead to her death. Some people have taken the Word of God for granted like the words of men. A man was telling someone that one does not have to be too quiet for people to talk to him anyhow and get away with it. He said, be vigilant with them; if it calls for fight, fight them and when you are done, ask God for forgiveness and He is merciful to forgive you.

He said he did that to people that tried that with him and they know that he is always ready for war if they ask for it but he forgot that sin that is repeated is called *"**iniquity**",* and it is abomination to God; and God does not pay attention to it. Anyone that can lie can also steal, this is the area the devil comes in because he is a liar, thief and killer; he tried it on Job through his friends (Bildad, Zophar, and Eliphaz), he also tried to use Job's wife against Job, so he can curse God and die because he is a man of integrity.

Job didn't give up on God but resisted the devil; and thank God for another of his friends, the youngest amongst them called "Elihu" whom God used to restore confidence in Job; and God spoke with him and blessed him. You may say that money didn't give you chance to serve God, then be ready to see Job, who God blessed and never gave excuses to serve God and God vouched for him; even the devil also knew that Job was a good man that feared God and never sinned against God. You say you are poor that's why you did not serve God, then be ready to see Lazarus because he was poor and never choose to navigate his way to get wealth but served God in all righteousness: Even Jabez went through a life of emptiness and he cried unto God and his story was changed to glory by God.

You may say that you are not educated then; please be ready to see Peter, the apostle of Jesus Christ. You want to give excuse that you are a politician, then be ready to face Joseph, because he was a Prime Minister in Egypt and he served God in truth and spirit. Lying will never help anyone nor pave way for you, because it chases helpers far from you, ridicule you; it will disgrace you and make you feel embarrassed in public, for it is like the word that says: *"Every day for the thief, one day for the owner".* Too much of debate cause one to lie because God is against it, you argue from now till tomorrow and it changes nothing because they are all lies; you see many people gathered at where newspaper stands or where people are gathered to debate and argue on politics, sports and so on because such people blame others for their failures; and when they go back home, they lie to their relatives, wives, husbands and others that the day is not as good as they expected it.

Meanwhile they neither go to work nor look for one but choose to remain in one place and argue about all things and if such people are given chance they won't do anything because they can say Heaven and Earth and fulfill nothing: Some others are busy using people's brain to enrich themselves posing to be servants of God but not the one and only true God; but the devil because he lives in them; they tell you to get coconut and use it to round your head with your own hands and your problems will be solved; some will tell you to go and have bath in the river and your problems will be solved: It is just like the one I heard people talk about some time ago, it amazes me because I have never heard that phones capture angels which is a deep and big lie of the highest order.

The reason why their tricks and lies are being played well on their hearers is because they are miracle seekers; some of them do not like to pray and fast because they consider it time wasting and to them time is money, which means they love money more than life but they don't know that life is God. They can pay someone to help them fast and pray when they are supposed to do it themselves because in their heart or thought God is a magician but they will use wiles of the devil in them to convince you that it is faith but it is all lie.

# #6: COVETOUSNESS

This is an act or habit of greed or not being satisfied or not contented. The word ***"covetousness"*** is a very bad character in a Christian's life and it may lead to bewitchment and also make one put on an unwanted character that does not reflect Christ. In Isaiah 14:12-15, the Bible tells us of Lucifer, how he tried to dethrone God and enthrone himself because of greed in him, Despite the love God showed him but he wasn't satisfied with it but chose to wrestle against his creator. Covetousness moved Gehazito run after Naaman when his master, Elisha said he doesn't want anything from Naaman; but Gehazi never tried to ask his master why neither groomed himself in God's word that say there is time for everything (see, Ecclesiastes 3).

Covetousness has led many into uncalled relationship which brings unwanted pregnancy and also rejection because of lust for material things. When you believe you can maneuver your way into having or getting riches but unfortunately it turned out bad for you. Covetous has led many into what they are not called or ordained to be but the work of lust in them called "covetousness" has turned them to something else, mostly young girls and boys, some are still in primary and secondary schools; even those that are sent to school by their parents or sponsored by someone else, yet they go and mess up themselves because of lack of contentment.

Covetousness is what makes some people to be against others for their breakthroughs, success, and promotion; and want to pull them down because they are very eager to get what you have but still neither contented nor wait on God for a better tomorrow. Lack of contentment caused the Children of Israel not to get to the Promised Land on time: The Lord wanted it to be forty days journey and also warn them not to provoke Him through sin and that the spirit of Egypt in them should be taken off them - they never listened but were asking and demanding and never changed from it but transgressed against God and the journey of forty days became forty years because of their lust of Covetousness, they transgressed against God and were punished for it.

Covetousness made Saul, the son of Kish to sin against God when he was told by Samuel,the servant of God to obey the words of the Lord but Saul went and did his own bidding because he gave himself to lust after material things, he failed to destroy some of the things God commanded him to destroy. He came back and lied to the servant of God and he received curse because his sin was revealed and he tore the garment of the servant of God and the Spirit of the Lord departed from him and an evil spirit possessed him. Even in churches, you see someone who just started church not too long, aiming for post that he is not called to hold but the greed in him/her will push him/her to do whatsoever even if it means going for fetishes to acquire that position, he/she will do it. And when it backfires on him/her then they begin to seek for God and His forgiveness.

Covetousness made David to go after Uriah's wife and also killed him, when he refused to go in unto his wife. David wrote a letter and gave it to Uriah to hand it over to Joab to read it and Joab understood the message and put Uriah in front of the battle and no one supported him and he died by the sword of the enemies and the word of the Lord came to David by the servant of God called Nathan and he received curse that sword will never depart from his house. It is written in the Lord's commandments that *"covet not thy neighbor's wife".* No matter the situation of any family, if you are in a position to help, do help and God will bless and reward you but never use that as an opportunity to make out with thy neighbor's wife because the wrath of God will never depart from you; after all, the Bible has shed more light to the life of its ups and downs; so it will be better for one to know how to walk in life.

But one cannot know it all because it is written: *"forsake not the gathering of the saints"*, it is better to go to church and worship God there with the people gathered there whether they are good or bad, let God be the judge and not you. Just like some people say *"I don't have to go to church to be called a Christian because I am better than them, but it is only one thing that is pulling me back";* and that thing is lust which you covert after, and it can only be taken off you by Jesus not by yourself because without Him, you can do nothing. And note that when you are guilty in one thing, you are guilty in all, so says the word of the Lord. Do not always think that you are better in one thing when you are guilty in another thing; which means you are guilty of all. Gomer, Prophet Hosea's wife was lustful because she has wandering eyes which is the same as

Covetousness, and that made her to cheat on her husband but thank God that her husband has the fear of God and that made him grow in the Spirit of God, in wisdom, knowledge and understanding. He did not put her away meaning that he did not divorce her, but learnt that God has been tolerating adulterous life in His people of Israel, but that did not make Him to forsake His people but He loved them more because He is love: That made Hosea to win his wife back and purchased her freedom; and that made her to serve God in truth and spirit.

Covetousness will make parents to force their children to go astray like telling them go into prostitution, internet fraud or to even steal just to acquire wealth and for their desire to be met - it is ungodly. It's just like the story of a young boy, I heard when he said he was in Senior Secondary School whereas his own father took him to guys that are engaged in internet fraud like scamming people, which they call “YAHOO” and since then his life has become something else and still he is thanking his father because he showed him the way to success but his behavior is zero and lacks manner of approach and what most of them don't know is what they are doing is like a wood eaten by termites. The reward is laziness and it will be too late to come back because the years that the locust has eaten cannot be restored except you quickly turn to God that can do all things. He does not forsake anyone but delivers and makes one's burden to be light and yoke to be easy. He is just to forgive you and take you back because He is love. He will be with you at every point of the way.

Later some will say that the Bible is not telling the truth or it is not making sense, when the Bible tells us that on the 'Last Days' mother shall be against the daughter, mother-in-law shall be against daughter-in-law; father shall be against the son, father-in-law shall be against the son-in law.

Wake up and pray because all that glitters are not gold and have the fear of God which is the beginning of wisdom. It just like a rich man that I saw who sent boys to block the way and collect money from every bus and bike that pass bye because he wants to repair one place or the other on the road. Covetousness will make a comedian that is void of the knowledge, wisdom, understanding of God to come to church and start telling jokes even when the church invites him to come and tell joke because the fear of God is not in his/her life, but love money: He / She will hearken to their call and when it backfires on them in one way or the other then will you know that God is the head of principalities and powers, and He does not joke with His word or work. If He can do it to the Children of Israel when they were doing business in His Father's House in Jerusalem and He rebuke them and said to them

> *"my father's house is a house of prayer, not a den of thieves or a house of merchandise"*(Matthew 21:13; Mark 11:17).

Parents that encourage their children to leave their marriage because of their selfish interest are not helping them but hindering the progress of God in their lives. And you, the children that your parents or friends are telling to quit your marriage should not hearken nor listen to them because they didn't leave theirs, even when their husbands are not doing well but remain in the marriage, if you want to be successful, commit your ways and life into the hands of God and not covet because you want quick riches, so you won't regret your action or steps you took for the success; and life is determined by God and ***"He holds the key of your life"***.

# #7:BACKSLIDERS

These are people who go back to the world and please the world in every worldly ways after they have believed. Backsliders are the ones that easily give up on Christ and follow the ways of the world because they feel there is nothing profitable in following Christ. Some of them will tell you that poverty is a thing of the mind and only a fool will be running to church and pray when he/she supposed to go and get busy with their lives. Those that say such things are the real fools because the Bible tells us *"if the foundation be destroyed what can the righteous do?"* (Psalm 11:3). Most of them you hear talking like that, their parents have paid the price for them while working with God and the doors and windows of Heaven are opened to them; but because they are void of the things of God which are His ways, that's why they talk like that not knowing that there are two ways the devil play his wiles on them, which are; to make them continue to have riches and speak negatively about God and to please the world or make them crumble because that is the work of his hand, an enemy of progress.

Nobody is told the truth anymore and the word ***"truth"*** is God, everyone is too busy running here and there to earn a living by their own strength, which is not right. Success is determined by God, and it can be achieved by obeying Him and worship in truth and spirit. One with God is more than a thousand; so it is not a must to be like the worldly ones, be contented with God; for he that is faithful in little shall be faithful in many. Speaking of those that say; 'poverty is a thing of the mind'. If one watches their children or their homes very well, it is not as one thinks it will be because there is no God in their midst or in their home. Backsliders are seen everywhere in the church, homes, schools, and even in the society because they are used by the devil to mislead others to go astray, but they still claim to be Christians. When you see some in the church dressed like they are there to showcase themselves, some wear clothes that are revealing the body, maybe they are there to tempt others, some are there to do nigga or big boy or big girl, some are there to devour others with their Sugar-coated words and make out with them.

Mind you, it is not every one that comes to church are really Christians because some are there to lead you to the other side of life which is not Godly but ungodly and that is to make the devil mock God in your life. Some are there to lead others astray because they know those that are miracle seekers and they will tell you they know one Baba that can solve your problems, and like a fool, you follow him/her to see the Baba and your life becomes problematic for you to bear because you did not find God where He can be found. I can still remember a story my economics teacher told us back then at school and what he also said afterward; he said there is a boy that was very ill, and he had bruises on him, his parents were seeking for help and they have been going to and fro to get help and they are Christians but nothing happened nor work for them, then they met someone that told them of a Native Doctor who told them that he has power to heal people. They followed him to where the man, the Native Doctor was. When they got there, the Native Doctor never asked for any money but told them to get him clothes like white one and they should leave the rest to him.

Then they gave it to him, and as he used the clothes on the boy, the Native Doctor swallowed it, and finally, the boy was healed but another battle began for him because the Native Doctor wants the boy but his parent never agreed because they believed that what brought them to him was over and they have settled it, but the Native Doctor made them to remember that he didn't take anything from them and that was how the battle started. But there was a statement my economics teacher made; while the boy and his parents were desperate to get him healed, he said *'If you are waiting on God to heal you, and he didn't answer you, you are free to go to small gods for healing and it will not be counted sin for you because God knows he did not answer you'.* Thank goodness that some of us then did not hearken to him because he was trying to convince us that it is the way, although he is matured but like they say *'age is just a number'* and if it is by age to walk with God, then God could not have talked to Samuel when he was young while Eli was there, but He did not speak to Eli but Samuel because the children of Eli did evil in the sight of God; but Eli never talked to them nor scolded them but said *"let God do what is right in His sight",* and that made him to lose his children to the sword of the enemies and he also died as well because he fell from where he was sitting. Notwithstanding, he received curse that no one will grow old in the lineage of his father's house. Thank God, the economics teacher hearkened to us that were not in agreement with what he said and he said 'our faith is very strong' because he did not expect us to be bold to confront him, that it is not right. I could remember the day, I met a man that was telling me of God while he was misquoting the Bible; he gave me some portions of the Bible to read and that when I am done reading it, I should come and see him. I gave him mine as well and he read mine but I didn't read his because he is not a Christian but the opposite of Christianity. I set about going to him, but when he saw me from afar he ran away from where he was and never came back.

It was backsliders that told Rehoboam, the son of Solomon, the son of David, the son of Jesse, to maltreat the people because his father (Solomon) was very calm with them and he should not be calm with them but to be very hard on them. God loves David, that is why He did not take away the whole kingdom from him, but left two tribes for his son to rule; and the other ten tribes were given to Jeroboam; he later did evil in the sight of God and died shamefully. Some will tell you that it was the demon in the sea that possessed Moses, that's why he didn't reach the Promised Land but they forget that the word says *"God will never share his glory with anybody"*(Isaiah 42:8):*Or* light and darkness can never meet because when light appears, darkness fade away.

The Bible did not tell us anything like that but he has anger in him, even God called him a **"meek man"** and also said there is none like Moses on Earth. God never said the devil possessed him but hindered him from entering the land of promise. He had prepared for the people of Israel a land that flows with milk and honey because of his love. Even Some say 'it is fornication that Adam and Eve committed, and that is why God sent them out of the garden of Eden and it is not only fruit they ate, you can also eat with other part of your body, which is sex': I laughed when I heard them talk like that because the Bible tells us that after God created them in His own image and likeness, He blessed them and said *"be fruitful, multiply, and replenish the earth"* (Genesis 1:28). He wanted them to have seeds upon the Earth and also have dominion over it and He also called them "man and wife" because He is the one that joined them and He is the Author and Source of Marriage.

Backsliders will always complain of everything and they will also say *'it is impossible to do without sin'* but forgetting that the Name of the Lord is a Strong a Tower, the Righteous runs into it and he is save; the Bible also tells us that "*in the name of Jesus, every knee must bow, every tongue must confess that JesusChrist is lord"*(Romans 14:11; Philippians 2:11). Backsliders are the ones you find putting their trouser at their buttocks; they are the same that have tattoo on their body even if they have the name of our Lord Jesus on their skin, but that does not make one a better person or righteous with God. They are the ones that serve God with tradition and still compare the one and only true God with other gods that are the handiwork of men or false religion, inviting comedians to church because the House of God is a court of jesting for them; and not a house a prayer because of their lustful desire. They are the ones that encourage you to do the negative because of their lust for the world, having the love of money than God but never make impact in the world: They are void of understanding of the things of God, the poor are useless to them; those that pray are too local to them when they attain riches, which God make it possible for them.

# #8 WORSHIPPERS OF IDOL

These are people who use their time and effort to create images for themselves and for their use and purpose. In other words it is an image made by man in order to subdue people to satanic covens. In Exodus 20:3-4, God is against serving an image or idol because He said *"I am a jealous God"* which tells us that God is very humble because He brings Himself too low to us by telling us His likes and dislikes; and He is also jealous of seeing what He created in His own image after His likeness to worship what have no mouth to speak, nose to smell, ear to listen; nor eyes to see.
There was a man called Jeroboam in the Bible, whom God made to be king over Israel, because of the sin of Solomon and his son, Rehoboam; but Jeroboam sinned against God, even God knew that He would sin against Him but told Jeroboam saying; if he will worship Him in truth and spirit, He, God will bless him and prosper his ways, but Jeroboam did not listen to the voice of God: He went and built an altar for idols or the graven images, made by himself to worship: The Bible tells us that those who made them are just like them.

Some trust in idols and fetish powers but a true child of God will trust the Lord because a child of God's help comes from the Lord who made the Heaven and the Earth; He has all the power and it belongs to Him. The Bible tells us that Jeroboam didn't change his ways and the wrath of God came upon him and his son fell sick, then he knew that only God can heal his son for him; but unfortunately he got what he deserved because one can't maneuver his way into the presence of God and think God will overlook it, forgetting that God is very just in His ways and not partial.

Are you a Pastor that seek for powers from other sources not called by God but the devil and you are using the power of devil to heal people but still afflicting them the more and putting them in bondage. Do you think you are trying to help God, when it is written in the book of Isaiah that

> *"the hand of the lord is not shortened to save neither is his ear heavy for him to hear you but your iniquity have separated you from God"*(Isaiah 59:1).

For you to know that the devil is really working and not on his own like other people claim to say he is; you find some youth using demonic power to put others in bondage because they belong to cult. Some use it for their political ambition and they see human beings to be nothing, some use it to manipulate others to lose their wealth and become nothing which they call ***'yahoo'*** and it is a fraudulent act and ungodly.

Like I was told by my pastor, some years ago, he said something about young boys that are used by God to worship Him in truth and spirit: That whenever they pick up the microphone to sing praises to the Lord,
everyone feel the presence of God but after a while they gave up on God because they are not patient with Him to wait for their own time; and also prayed more for God to direct their steps. But now they have engaged in ungodly act because they have gone to seek powers from other sources and they call

themselves ***'prophets and prophetess'*** but my pastor called them and warned them not to continue with it lest they regret their actions, but they did not listen to him.

Eventually, nemesis caught up with them and they were crumbled despite the power they seek from the devil and he made mockery of them because he has come to steal, kill and to destroy; that was what he did with them and made them what the word of God says *'the glory of God has departed'*, which is **"Ichabod".** But, they forget that all that glitters are not gold: What God has not ordained is uncalled for and not pleasant to Him because He knows all things and can do all things. He knows the Best time for everyone because some their foundation is not good and there are yokes, burdens and barriers that need to be broken for one to attain success in life and to shine the light of God to the world for them to know that God really exist.

The Idol worshippers use valentine day celebrating as an opportunity to have illicit relationships with ladies and men and it is the work of the devil; Christmas that is supposed to be for our Lord Jesus, to celebrate Him and glorify Him with Godly activities, but we have turned it to worldly ways.

# #9: SERVING GOD AND MAMMON

This means a being trying to serve two masters at the same time. John 4:24, tells us that God is a Spirit and He must be worshipped in truth and spirit, not with Mammon because He is greater, and not worship of mammon because it is not good. God is good all the time; and He is patient but does not take chances; He is love (John 3:16), He is the great giver because He does not think twice before giving and without condition does He give; He blessed Solomon beyond his imagination when he asked for wisdom to rule the people of God, Israel; He blessed Jabez when his mother said *"He is more honorable than his brethren but he was in sorrow"* (1Chronicles 4:9); and Jabez cried unto God and his reproach was taken off him to the glory of God. He made David, a shepherd boy to rule His people, Israel.

You don't serve God for material purpose but for Eternity and to be saved from the damnation that is to come, for in the presence of God there is fullness of Joy and yokes are broken; one shall be free from affliction, pain and agony, trials and temptation for His word says on ease lies the head that wears the crown. Do not allow your so much desire for success or material things take the best of you but let God have the best of you because you exist in Him, in Eternity and He made you exist to make impact in life and fulfill His agenda here on Earth, and also you are god as well because you are made in His own image after His likeness.

To serve God does not mean one won't face ups and down of life which others called ***'trials and temptation'*** but always remember before the world hate you or persecute you, it persecuted Jesus and He overcame it because He loves us and took our sin upon Himself and with Him on your side, you will overcome. He was with Joseph and never left him alone and prospered him in the land of his affliction and he was made second-in command over Egypt. Like I said before, Lord Jesus said *"You can't serve two masters at the same time, is either you love one and hate the other"* (Matthew 6:24). It's either you love God and hate the other or you love Mammon and hate God.

When you love Mammon, it means you donot love God because you have the love of money, material things and carnal ways. I have heard and seen people who claim to love God but placed Him beneath their needs because their needs must always come first, when the Bible says *"seek ye first the kingdom of god and his righteousness and all other things will be added unto you" (Matthew 6:33).* The love of Mammon have lead many astray which is bad because they don't have Jesus and neither can they preach the word of God in truth and in spirit because they can't give what they do not have. Someone said there is a guy he knows that is into fraudulent business like ***'internet fraud'****,* but when he preaches the word of God to people, they listen attentively to him but at the same time, he is engaged in sin and there is no sign of change or remorse in the people's live that he preached to because he can't give what he does not have – that's Jesus. Some are told to use what they have to get what they want which is very bad and uncalled for because it is the will of the devil to destroy one from God's promises, some don't want to work because of the title they bestow upon themselves which is 'I am a graduate', I cannot be seen doing jobs that are not up to my qualification. Which is not an encouraging word but makes them deviate and violate the Temple of God which is your body through fornication and adultery but the reward that comes with it is very painful. The Bible says *"the wages of sin is death"* and it also says *"anyone that destroy the temple of God, will God destroy"* and it also says, *"fornication/adultery is a sin against the body and soul":*So, it will be better for one to be very careful and the word of God also says *"be careful for nothing"* because your adversary, the devil is going about looking for whom to devour. You are not called to worship the world but God because of the task given to you is to glorify Him in every way - minutes, seconds, hours, and every moment of your life. You are here to make impact in people's lives not by material things alone but with the word of God to revive souls to be on fire for God and to be in the Holy Ghost because without the great comforter, the Holy Spirit of God, one cannot excel.

# #10: HATRED

This is an act that dissects good things, good character and behavior. Mostly, these are the kind of people that blame others for their failures but forget God or put Him out of the picture. Hatred breeds bitterness and envy (see, Job 1:6-11), for the devil hated the stand of Job because God vouched for him to be perfect, upright, one that fear God and eschewed evil. Hatred is also known to be murder before God and it is a fruit of doom from the pit of hell where the devil inhabits. Like they say *'If nobody talks about you, then you are nobody, whether it is true or lie, they tell about you'.* If you live a good and Holy life, people will *always* complain of you and if you live or lead a bad life, people will still talk so it is vice-versa; it just like a movie I watched and I saw these words written *'A man in life without challenge is like a joker'*: Don't feel or be surprised that people, even your closest friend and relative hates you.

Hatred will make you misunderstand people for what they are not and can make you have blood-stain on your hands through lies and unfaithfulness to one another. Sometimes, it can be when ones feeling is not reciprocated, then hatred sets in, which comes through lust but not love because the word "Love is God". There is no hatred in God but love, and the things He hate the most is sin. It is very possible for one to do without sin because God is greater than it: He took human form and still overcame sin though He said *"The Spirit is willing but the flesh is weak* "(Matthew 26:41; Mark 14:38); yet, that is not an excuse to sin and with Him by your side, you will overcome and overtake because He is your Helper. But when one tries to do everything in his/her own way and it does not work out but it does for another person, please don't blame God or anyone but watch and pray: Give thanks to God because it is written: *"In all things give thanks to God"* and see things turn around for your good because the blessing of the Lord makes rich and adds no sorrow.

The devil is a thief that's why the Bible tells us that he has come to steal, kill and destroy (John 10:10). So, don't let devil have his way in you by making you to hate others for your misfortune, sometimes it can be our parents that failed to walk with God in truth and spirit like others because they choose to maneuver their way onto the top and now it has backfired on you. Now, you are trying to regain all that were lost but it seems difficult; it will be better for you to walk with God, not for yourself but for your generation like Abraham, Isaac, Jacob (Israel), Joseph, Moses, Joshua, Samuel, Nathan, Isaiah, Job, Ezekiel, Deborah, David and many more, including the disciples of our Lord Jesus and they affect lives and even their children walked with God to please God: And their lives never remain the same again but transformed in the glory of God. Don't be like the Pharisee that exalted himself before God and condemned the Publican and the Bible made it clear that the prayer of the Pharisee was not answered but God had respect to the prayer of the Publican becausehe knew he is not worthy to come into the house of God.

Hatred made Cain to kill Abel because Cain gave sparingly to God while

Abel gave bountifully to God; and God respected Abel's offering and that made Cain to kill him. Hatred made Esau to try to kill Jacob because he foolishly sold his birthright to Jacob. As a result, Cain despised his twin brother, Abel to the point of killing him. Hatred made the world to hate Jesus because He is the way, the truth and the life; and no one comes to the Father but by Him. Hatred made them to kill Jesus because He was telling them the truth: The enemy of the truth resides in the world, and in the heart of those that love destruction - that enemy is the devil, the father of liars and master of deception. The truth tells us that those that lose their lives for His name's sake shall find it; but those that love their lives shall not find it. You see the truth and tell it, someone else will aim for your life because they love darkness and dwell in it.

The more you try to kill the truth, the more it will fight back at you and it will also affect you because you are causing yourself more trouble and allowing the devil and his cohorts to have a say over the truth, and those that are walking in it to deviate from Him. After all, the Bible made it clear to us about the tree in the Garden of Eden which is *"the tree of knowledge of good and evil and the tree of life".* The Tree of Knowledge of Good and Evil is telling us that God made good and evil; and at the same time, Satan, the devil is evil and hate good things, he also wants to rule, that's why he tempted the woman because he saw her weaknesses and used it against her and she ate the fruits of tree and also gave to the man (Adam) to eat as well and they both did and that was how sin started upon the Earth. Because the devil wants to rule and have dominion over what God created. Hatred made the devil to do that because first, he tried to dethrone God and enthrone himself as god, but he was cast down from Heaven to Earth and God said *"woe to the inhabitants of the earth for Lucifer has come with a great wrath for he has a short time"*(Revelation 12:12).

Thank God for Jesus, who came and overcame the devil and set us free from his wiles, tares, evil deeds and temptation of the devil and every other ways of his to manipulate and pull one down from where God wants him/her to be, all the hatred in him which is bitterness. The Tree of Life is God and that is the word of God. The word of God is Life and light unto our path: The Tree of Life is Salvation, Eternal Life; it delivers from the will of Satan. It makes you live forever, it is the Fruit of the Spirit that brings life not death. It is good and it breeds love and Godliness, that's God.

# #11: FIGHTING

This is an act that comes through quarreling, arguing, malice and hatred. Genesis 4:8, tells how fighting brought hatred between two brothers including envy. If Cain had given bountifully to God, his offering would have been respected and accepted but he gave sparingly while his brother (Abel) gave to God bountifully and his offering was accepted and respected by God but it made Cain envious of Abel and fought against him to death. All these wiles of the devil came from the act of disobedience to God, right from the Garden of Eden. Adam and Eve have ears to listen to simple instructions from God but no, they didn't but gave in to the words of a serpent, which is the devil; and evil had its way into the world. What supposed to be obtained with ease; one have to fight a good fight to have it because your adversary, the devil is always ready to see you crumble, in life: The only way he can be defeated is through prayer and the Lord says "*hold your peace and I will fight for you*" (Exodus 14:14).

Those who take blood in their hands because they want to avenge for themselves are not helping the matter but also committing sin by killing their fellow human beings just like a religion preaches *'If you kill an infidel or Christian, you have wives in heaven which are pure'*, but that is all lie because there is no such thing as man and wife in heaven. The Holy Spirit in you, is the Kingdom of God in you, the Spirit of God teaches you all things because He is **"The Comforter"** - all things are committed to the Spirit of God, the Holy Ghost that comes from the Father and helps you defeat the devil. The devil and his cohorts, the enemies of God are not holy but unholy, they work hard to make you stand firm against the ways of God: The same God that prepared David to defeat Goliath; the same God that strengthened Samson against the Philistines and their demonic gods called Dagon; the same God that raised Moses for Pharaoh, so that His people will be delivered from bondage to serve Him in the Land which He prepared for them, a land flowing with milk and honey. That's why the Bible says: *"pray without ceasing*", and always commit your ways to God. The devil won't have way into your life; he will surely be put to shame same way the Lord Jesus did to him by finishing the work on the Cross of Calvary. A good Christian fights on his/her knees with prayer and not to faint nor cease from it: God will fight the battle for you, for whatever you bind on Earth shall be bound in Heaven, and whatever you loose on Earth, shall be loosed in Heaven. Vengeance is of the Lord, leave it for Him to avenge for you through your zeal for Him and His kingdom; also, He loves you, and He will not fail because He has never lost the battle.

# #12: FROWARD TONGUE

A mouth filled with lies and dangerous words that can lead to trouble. Froward tongue is the mouth that causes trouble, problem and demonic attack from the coven of demonic world. Genesis 4:9-12, describes how froward tongue made Cain to receive curse from God. It tells us that we should have manner of approach because the mouth that lacks manner gets worst and terrible things as reward. The words of the people of Sodom and Gomorrah made them to lose their sight when the Angels of God came to see the wickedness of Sodom and Gomorrah and it brought their destruction and doom. In Genesis 25:30-31, we read how a forward mouth is filled with stupidity and useless words and how it can make one to provoke his/her neighbor. This is the kind of mouth that can sugarquote words to mislead people to the wrong path of life, which can be seen as lies just as the devil did to Eve not minding what God told Adam about the fruit of the tree of life, but they gave in to the words of the enemy that his major aim is to steal, kill and destroy.

Any person with froward tongue will try to convince you that fornication is not sin because there is always a first time for everything in life, that even those doing it are still living and not dead, and by the way, God is merciful and will always forgive even when one just commit sin for the first time, or there is no harm in trial – that's the conclusion of a forward mouth trying to convince you into sin. Many are under satanic attack and demonic bondage as a result of their froward tongue, the same way Pharaoh was trying to negotiate with Moses by telling him to leave the young children of Israel to stay and go with the old ones but Moses did not agree because the Lord commanded him to go with everyone and all their belongings to serve Him (God) in the land that flows with milk and honey. A froward mouth will tell you big lies that you are not matured enough even though you are of matured age because you are not involved in illicit way of living; that is why you are not matured or growing, but he/she forgets that growth is defined *'as someone who increase in size and quantity'* not by sex, for sex before marriage is sin and it's forbidden.

A froward tongue easily change like Chameleon because they are not truthful but deceitful in ways which are not Godly but worldly. Their ways are evil, unpleasant because it makes one move from sorrow to sorrow and from grace to grass. They choose to serve God according to their own terms and no one tells them what to do because they claim to know everything. Someone was talking to me some time ago; he said I should sit down and listen to him because he wants to tell me all about life. He said this life is not how people take it to be, because he has seen a lot in life and no one can tell him what to do and not to do even if it be a pastor because they have used theirs to deceive many: That life is all about give and take, then he said something about where he worship because he claims to be Christian, and he said the parish priest where he worships goes here and there and the members do not know when he is going out of the country but when they changed their parish priest; then he pulsed abruptly and changed the topic to church politics: He talked about other pastors and how they mislead people because they are not called and are lazy to work, how they use their brain to deceive people to enrich themselves and they are not far from being called a thief. I was just looking at him because he does not know that the few minutes I spent with him, God made me to know the kind of person he is, his type are many in the church and society at large and they are called ***'commentators and spectators'*** Like the Bible tells us of how Lucifer was cast out of Heaven because of his forward tongue and God cast him out of Heaven, although he was not the only one because he and some other angels in accord with him were cast out together.

And many fell in different places and their desire since then is to lead people astray: They are still in one accord with the devil which is to steal, kill and destroy. To steal means to deceive you through the wiles of the devil to abort the glory of God in your life and place a forbidden fruit in your life. To kill means to tie down one's spiritual life of praying and fasting in other to be confused and make him/her fall the more into his trap. To destroy means he has successfully finished his aims and objectives and will over one's life and spirit; including aborting the good fruit God has bestowed on you and then take his/her soul to Hell, the world of doom.

Many Christians have practiced froward tongue character: These are enemies of God because He said in His word *"I love a truthful mouth but hate a froward mouth"* (Proverbs 8:13). The reason God hate a forward mouth is the lies and temptation that comes into the world through Satan, their master and he is full of deceit. Many that have such in them are those that are too boastful of themselves and say all sort of things that they will do; even to give glory, honor and praise to themselves instead of giving it to God, they choose to glorify themselves. These are the kind of people you find in the same spot or square one. A being with froward mouth can render you useless, by making you go into business that is not lucrative just to jilt you from your money/success and also likes to see you crumble. They lack the fear of God in them because they can do anything to achieve anything and will never use it to do something good because they believe you spend more and save less and when it doesn't favor them, they look for something odd to do like to deceive people and deprive them of their right, which is demonic. They are also known to be *'you know me, you dey do me; you dey do, you dey pity me'.*

# #13: PRETENDERS

These are those who claim to be true friends or Christians to you, but neglect you during the time of needs; and they are false philanthropists, also. The Bible passage in Job 4:8-9, tells us of how Eliphaz, the temanite accused Job of sin and that God is punishing him for his evil deeds but never prayed with him nor assisted him in any other way. Job's three friends did not help him because they were neither true Christians nor true friends; they were there only for the money and not to encourage him or to show him love. They were more like familiar friends because they were only there for what they could get from him, and also say negative things to him because they were envious of his success.

I know of a man that usually do something like that to people; once he gets to a place where he knows people, he spends the whole of the money with him, thank goodness that his late mother left a building for him and that covers his secret. But when things were not going as expected for him because people were expecting him to spend for them like before; he still did even know when he was to stop, and to take his stand so they can know that he was no longer financially buoyant, but he continued and said ***'we must show love to one another'*** until when one told him that he spends like a fool and the people he was spending for deviated from him when he had nothing. They called him names and he learnt his lesson in the hard way because he cannot please people always, no matter what.

The Bible tells us that upon all God did for the children of Israel; they were not satisfied because of their stiff-neck behavior. Even Economics says ***'human wants are unlimited';*** do not try to be what you are not but walk by the direction of the Holy Spirit. The story of the Pharisees and Publican tells us not to pretend but be what God wants us to be. The Pharisee went into the temple of God built by King Solomon to pray; he exalted himself and God neglected his prayer because he was full of himself, and also did eye-service in the house of God and called the Publican a sinner. The Publican came into the house of God and humbled himself and God hearkened to his prayer because he knew that he was not worthy to come into the house of God because of his wrong doing.

You are not rich but you act to be rich and you go around borrowing things to impress people, you are helping the devil to do more hurt to your destiny and life. Greater is He that is in you than he that is in the world because you are created by the good God whose thought towards you is for good and not evil to bring you to an expected end. When you are a pretender, it means the life you live is fake and also full of lies and the devil abides in you. You will give space to the fruits of doom to come upon your life and also affect others with it because you are wishing yourself backwardness but God wants you to move forward in life, you are busy copying the celebrities, you see on television.

Some their families are not rich but manage because they are praying for a better tomorrow but their children are not living a good life and helpers are running far from them because of their negative acts. Don't tell people what God has not called you to be because it is lie you are telling and you are likely to fall back to square one and face life in a difficult way. What makes many to engage in this act is lust and reprobate heart; this is why you see many leaving the house of God to another source of power not knowing that can even steal their God given talent from them because they are void of the knowledge of God. They lay bad foundation for themselves and their children, then hardship sets in and it goes from generation to generation, just as Lord Jesus said to pretenders in the Bible: who know how to do evil secretly

> *"he said woe unto you, Scribes and Pharisees, you know how to devour women but put on the garment of priesthood to get respect from the people"*(Matthew 23:14)**:**

These are pretenders even in the house of God, they hear you loud and clear preaching the Gospel but they are adamant. You see them in church doing all sort of evil, and ungodly acts; they do business as they don't read the Bible to see the destruction that befall the children of the prophets that didn't hearken to the word of God, which is the truth and life but they chose death: The painful part is that they never believed because they saw themselves breathing, but internally there is no peace and they can't have it and Christ has profited them nothing, and
God has gone farther from them.

# #14: A FRIEND

This is someone who sticks to you through the ups and downs (good and bad times) of life. That friend is Jesus because He is the beginning of your life and will never forsake you because He loves and He knows you, formed you, and you exist in Him in eternity. There are different kind of friends which are familiar friends and unfriendly friends. ***Familiar friends:*** These are the kind of people that get close to you to know all about you but guess what? They don't know all about you because only God knows you completely just like the friends of Job called Bildad, Zophar, Eliphaz and Elihu; amongst them all, there was one that held his peace when he was going through trials and temptation and that person is Elihu because he was the youngest amongst them and was filled with the Spirit of God while the rest condemned Job to what they knew he didn't commit but the bad spirit called ***'familiarity'*** was upon them and they did not know when to tell him what will comfort him but made mockery of him and spoke negatively about God.

You even see them in churches, you hear them tell you, we have been here for years and we know everybody; but the word of God does not have meaning to them even the Pastors they know, yet they never get blessed because of their familiarity while others are being blessed, they care not because they believe such is life. These are the kind of friends that eat with you, but never helped you when you are going through hard times: They will not believe you because they think you don't have to lack anything. They are like termites; they can eat from you but can't contribute to your life whether with words to encourage you, even when you seek advice from them: They will give you useless advice that would not be something meaningful. They never make impact in life but always want you to make bearing in their lives because they believe without you they cannot be what they want to be.

Many of them can do you hurt but still see it to be normal because they are too familiar with you as Judas Iscariot did to Lord Jesus and received curse; for it is written *"the son of man, goeth as it is written of him but woe unto that man who would betray him, for it would have been better, if he had not been born"* (Matthew 26:24). That was Judas Iscariot, and the devil used him because he was close to Jesus, one of His disciples and knows the signs and wonders He did: Judas also thought it was going to be like that and that was the moment the devil was waiting for and he got it and used him (Judas) till he was destroyed. It is not good to be too familiar with someone and you never know what might happen because you are not in his/her mind to know what he/she is going through; so be very careful. Familiarity can make you disobey the commandment and order given to you by God because you believe if you don't obey Him nothing will happen.

There are people who did so in the Bible and died because God did not come to their rescue: King Saul, the son of Kish died while he was at battle because he failed to destroy all the people God commanded him to wipe out; but he went there to do his own bidding, and he came back and lied to prophet

Samuel. The Lord exposed him and he pleaded for it but God has gone far from him; the devil possessed him and moved him to seek David's life to destroy him, but he was unable to get David, and finally planted destruction for his family. He killed the servants of God, forgetting what the Bible says: *"Touch not my anointed and do my prophet no harm"* (1Chronicle 16:22); but he did because he was seeking for David's life, and when David was opportune to lay his hands on him, the Spirit of the Lord rebuked him from laying hands on him because he (King Saul) is God's anointed King; and it is only God that can deal with His anointed, not man. After, Saul went to a witch for consultation because he needed to know whether he is going to have victory over his enemies in a battle and he was persuaded to eat with the witch and there it really came to pass that he and his family were going to perish by the sword of their enemies.

Unfriendly friends are those that never wish you well but stick with you and also ready to lead you astray from the purpose of God. These are the kind of friends that do not want to rise because they will always believe you will never care for them and since they don't know how to walk or move in life or make a meaning out of their lives, they put others in mischievous acts which they engage in. It's just like the word I heard from someone that said when he was in school, a friend of his wanted him to belong to a cult and he never listened until one day, he said to him that *Capon* wants to see him. Then he said to his friend that tried to bring him into the cult; well, since you don't want me to rest, let me tell you what you don't know of me. I belong to a cult as well, and I cannot leave mine and join another, but I invite you and your ***Capon***; and it will be held by midnight in a graveyard but the friend got scared when he heard what he has not heard before and flee from him but the truth is that he does not belong to any cult and there is no meeting at midnight in a graveyard: but used that as an excuse to push him away from his side, so he would not corrupt (the friend).

I could remember what two young boys were saying when I was writing my West Africa School Certificate Examination; we met in the Examination Hall and knew each other from there, but the words from their mouths made me flee from them because their aims are very bad. Despite they were too young then for such plans; one said to the other, I must go to school because I see people coming home with different gifts and items while they are still in school. He said further that he knows a guy that came from a wretched family, he is not working neither does he have any means of livelihood but the last time, he came home to visit his parents, he came with a car and the way he talks shows that I can be like him or better than him. I did not get the meaning of what he was saying until I heard the second one speak his mind; the second one said he knows the guy, there is another one where he lives, the same thing happens in their family but the day he came back from school, he came with a big phone worth a huge amount of money; then I knew that these boys are not going to school to study but to join cult to oppress people for their selfish desires.

These are the kind of people that are not making impact in life, they love death and destruction; they are what the Bible calls them, ***"wasters".*** It will be better to flee from them and never walk with them. They appear to be nice outside but inside, they are devils and the words they vomit from their mouth will tell you more of their thought towards you. Unfriendly friends made King Rehoboam, King of Israel, son of Solomon, son of David, the son of Jesse, to take wrong decision and make offensive statement to the people and the kingdom was divided, leaving only two tribes for him to rule because of David, his father. A musician said in his song concerning unfriendly friends, he said *'Those I am supposed to hate are those that I love, because, he believes them, and those he is supposed to love are those that he hates because he doesn't believe them'*

Another sang a song about unfriendly friends, he said *'when money dey, friends go dey; when money no dey, friends go, go'*! But only Jesus will stay because He was rich but became poor for our sake and took our iniquity upon Himself; though He knew not sin, neither had he any sin. His word is confidence and faithful because the Psalmist says *"Many are the affliction of the righteous but the lord delivers him from them all"*(Psalms 34:19). Another name for unfriendly friends is ***'worldly friends'*** and they engage in acts like drinking, smoking, stealing, lying, fornicating, tempting and gossiping. Their ways are unpleasant to God and they are not ready to take heed to His Word for their heart is as strong as stone. Most Christians are involved in this act because they never waited on God's timing and promise. Such Christians are very canal and their ways are the ***'broad way'*** because they love the world and they believe they are from the world, that's why they engage in the things of this world.

What kind of friends do you follow or engage yourself with because I know Jesus is the one and only true friend that will never lead you astray only if you are patient with Him because He is not supposed to talk to you, walk with you nor have anything to do with you; but He is humble and brings himself low for you, so you will not go astray or be deceived by the world and fall into destruction. Jesus is the good shepherd that lay down His life for His sheep – that's you. The Bible tells us that the Godhead is three in one, which are *"The Father, The Son, and The Holy Spirit".* Most people would get confused or get it twisted when they hear or see something like this: Well, with God's grace; let me explain it so it can be clear.

In the beginning, according to the book of Genesis; the Bible tells us that God made Heaven and Earth but the Earth was without form and void and darkness was upon the Earth. The spirit of the Lord moved upon the face of the water, that Spirit is the Holy Ghost. And the Lord said, let there be light and there was light, that Word and Light is Jesus (see, John 1:1-5). When I said He is a Father, Friend and God is as He said in His word: I am the Father of the fatherless and husband to the widow. He called Abraham His friend, He called Lazarus His friend and He also said anyone that walks diligently with Him, shall no more be called ***'servant'*** but ***'friend'***. He is God because He made Heaven and Earth. He created humans in His own Image: All power belongs to Him, and there is nothing too difficult for Him to do. He parted the Red Sea for the children of Israel to walk on dry land; He gave them victory over Jericho without so much stress because the way He brought down the wall of Jericho is so amazing with just the shout of glory, and the wall fell down flat. He fed thousands of people with five loaves of bread and two fishes; He brought Lazarus back from death to life: He walked on the Sea, and commanded the storm to be still; He cursed a fig tree, and healed the woman with the issue of blood; He healed one of His disciple's mother of fever, and cast out demons from people: He overcome death by rising from the dead on the third day as He said, and He is God; the Sovereign God.

# #15: UNCALLED RELATIONSHIP

This is a relationship that is not ordained by God but by man.Most Christians in the world society find themselves in this category of life because they are faithless and impatient with God's word and timing. Judges 16:1-9 teaches how the relationship between Samson and Delilah made him fell weak of his strength and the enemies afflicted him. The relationship they had was not ordained by God but by lust he had for Delilah; and the consequences he faced was very disastrous: The enemy heard that the only way they can bring him down from his strength was to cut his hair, which Delilah did but they were not interested in that hair of his but choose to take away his sight as they plucked off his eyes.

This is the work of the devil, in every uncalled relationship; he knows what to do to harm one's life and never allows one to fulfill destiny because he is here to steal (to abort glory), to kill (waster), and to destroy (condemn for ever) - this is the work of the devil. I could remember years back, before God inspired me to write down His revelations to me; a lady whose family is very rich approached me and she was feeling on top of the world because she bragged about how wealthy they were, and when she was done talking, she asked me for my reply; I told her *'I will think about it',* and she was like asking me whether I do know the meaning of what I just said to her. I said yes because you are acting as the man, and I am acting as the woman, but to be sincere I never wanted to be in any relationship because then I love football so much and I focused on it.

Today, I thank God because if I had given in to her consent then: I don't know what I would have become today neither will I have the opportunity to what God has given me to write as an inspiration from Him because He makes way, where there seems to be no way. Another scenario I faced recently was a lady that was looking at me like she is lust: I never gave her the opportunity of talking to me neither did I talk with her but held my peace and allowed God to take permanent and absolute control over my life. Though, she never stopped looking at her attitude, she even flaunts her body whenever she sees me but thank God for His goodness, grace and mercies for not letting me to give in to it because it was quite tempting. Then one day, I was ready to go to church and clean because I belong to the sanctuary group / technical crew; but on my way to church, I saw a woman that looks like her mother because she is a widow, picking plastic bottles on the road to sell, so she can sell it for her children to eat, then I thanked God for not allowing me to give in to the lady's quest because I would have done hurt to my life and destiny: For what will I gain from five minutes pleasure and pay a price that I cannot probably redeem in my life time, just as the children of Israel did when God told them to walk with Him to the Promised Land for forty-days but they didn't listen to Him, and He told them if they try to tempt Him, the journey will not be forty-days but forty-years.

They never hearkened to the truth and sinned against God and the journey of Forty-days became Forty-years. I don't want my life to be like that and I thank God for not allowing me to go into uncalled relationship with anybody but have a close relationship with Him because He loves me and want the best for me. Most married men and women engage in uncalled relationship because of the spirit of adultery in their life, and as I said before; this kind of people believe that it is impossible to do without sin, and Christ will profit them nothing. They easily forget the vows of marriage they made to each other on the Altar of God because it means nothing to them; it is just mere word to them. But the truth is you have sinned against your body and soul; the devil will have his way into your home to cause many woes there because he is an enemy of progress; for the word ***'marriage'*** is an institution ordained by God as a covenant and not a contract. The more you are unfaithful in marriage because you engage in uncalled relationship the more damages you cause yourself because you are not ready to bear the cross: It leads to divorce which they call broken homes and God is against it because He has bored our iniquity, so we need to bear one another as well which is to Love one another no matter the consequences.

I saw a post on Facebook of a lady, she was very excited because she wrote something on her post, she said she came to school (University) with few clothes and two sandals, but now she is living with Refrigerator, Dstv (Digital Satellite Television Decoder), Generator, and other things. If that child is there to study, she will not upload the rubbish on Facebook because that shows she has men that pay her bills and she is happy she is wrecking the home of people and comforting them with fornication but what she does not know is what she is doing to others will be done to her in the process of her life, which is called ***'karma'*** Any young lady that talks like that and does not feel remorse for her action has many men under her calls like lawyers, pastors, prophet, politicians, professors, lecturers, teachers, and so on. I know many will not believe or like to argue about it, but listen; when you see a woman fights somebody or quarrel, and she will threaten you with people she has affair with like those I mentioned before, then you know that she is a home breaker.

I heard one say that porn movie is not sin because they are meant for couples and they have to use it to satisfy each other, yet she claims to be a Christian but love iniquity and they practice it; that is why the word of God says *"By their fruit, you shall know them"* You see some getting married to different kind of men and still divorce them because they see marriage as clothes they change whenever they want even celebrities are doing it and majority follow their footstep because they see it to be normal, and they like it that way. You are warned not to get entangled with someone that is ready for marriage but for a fling for one night stand and when you get pregnant, he tells you to abort it because you are a murderer, and you have no human feeling; then you are devil's agent because you walk in accord with him but guess what; he does not love you but use you against your Maker and seek for your destruction, so that the devil can torment you in Hell: Hell does not sound so pleasing, it is a place of torment and it comes from within.

Some have even made it so normal that they engage in the act of Sodom and Gomorrah which is gay, homosexual, sex-doll, sex machine and every other act of the devil because they say they use it to pass time. They belittle the name of the Lord and He shall go farther from them because they have messed up the Temple of the living God within them. Some travel overseas to do such evil and come back to act like they are on top of the world; even claim that it is hard work, that made them to be rich, the word of God calls it *"vanity upon vanity, all is vanity"* (Ecclesiastes1:2). Some even sleep with animals to get money, because they have been reduced to animal level, some of them are called by animal names because they mate like them: That is why it is good for you to wait on God's timing and direction for your life and don't be too hasty than your shadow because it is written *'on ease lies the head that wears the crown'.*

Rededicate your life back to God and deviate from every known and unknown sin. Mothers that encourage their children to go into uncalled relationship for their selfish desires are not far from being called a witches; even when it be the fathers that are doing same to their children, they are as well to be regarded as wizards because no one forced them when they were of their children age to do such; and even if they were, they are not supposed to do such to their children because the Bible says *"if a wicked man knows how to give good gift unto his children, how much more will your heavenly father do to you"*(Matthew 7:11). So, it will be better you don't train your children according to the ways of the world but God's way; for a wise man will train his children in the way of the Lord and they shall not depart from it.

One of the reasons most parents do not profit anything from their children is because they failed to lead their children to God, though they prayed for the children to succeed but forgot to dedicate them to God and allow God to be the Lord of their children's lives but forget put God aside. They put God aside and want their children to be rich so that when the success comes, the children will give their parents sparingly and sow more into the world where they will never reap. They have allowed the spirit of Mammon to gradually becloud their thoughts; the devil has his way in the lives of their children to bring them down to square one because he knows the kind of sin to push one to and he has his agents everywhere because he is not omnipotent, omnipresent nor omniscient: He does not want anyone to progress nor become what God wants one to become.

I could remember what I heard a guy say of his life; he said there was a time, he was doing well in life but unfortunately he kept the lady he wanted to marry in his apartment and kept buying her things just to make her happy and feel at home even when he was warned by a servant of God, but he did not listen, but later things were not going smoothly for him yet he continued and never gave up because he believes life is like that; sometimes you either win some or lose some, but he never knew that the lady he kept in his apartment was an agent of the devil because she was possessed by the devil: the lady started fighting and one day, she told him to his face that she is done with him and there is nothing good that can come out of him. She left him and ever since then life has not been fair to him because he listened to her word but looked down on God; and forgot that He is the yoke breaker and He has the final say over one's life.

Some are easily broken down because their girlfriends left them for another and they give themselves to alcohol, to sexual desire, and make themselves nuisance to the world because of a woman; even the same applies to women that do the same thing when their boyfriend leaves them for another lady. When somebody tells you, he wants to be your boyfriend it means he is just your male friend no strings feeling is attached because he is your friend not lover or sex mate. But this generation of today uses that as an excuse to commit immorality and to be satisfied by it while hurting their destiny. I watched a video on Instagram, where a lady was saying that it is not bad if your boyfriend beats you, it is just to show that he loves you and he does not want you to be misled by someone else or see you go astray; that is why he beats you. She also said her boyfriend beats her, because he loves her and wants the best for her: What a foolish thing to say; it does not make sense for someone that is not your husband to beat you, even your husband does not have the right to beat you but to dwell with you according to the knowledge of God. A woman is like a nation filled with different kinds of character, and one can only dwell with her through perseverance; mostly with the knowledge of God through the Fruits of the Spirit (see, Galatians 5:22-23). Some even use charm to sleep with women because that is the only thing they have at heart and mind; no plan for their lives and when they see their mates progressing, they say he/she is raising shoulder for them.

Lord Jesus is the Rock, many or few Christians that want their lives to be better and prosper, are standing in Him because He never fails. In every relationship there is something called *'love and respect'* for one another, there is nothing like a woman's place is in the kitchen because she is your Help-meet, not your slave. Woman, respect your husband whether you are doing better than him or not; and use good words to encourage each other not to curse one another neither fight each other nor make one feel inferior. Do not use your certificate to boast at each other because marriage is bigger and greater than that - the certificate is the work of men not God: And to those women that run to men's house because of what they have and profess love to you, that does not mean you should throw yourself at him, stop the mess-endowed life you are living, respect yourself and honour God, if you want people to respect you because if you don't and you give yourself to a man that has not paid your bride price or wed you, then your name is sorry because you gave yourself cheaply to him and he may not marry you; and if he does then he may be going out to commit adultery behind you. The way I see how young girls give themselves to men makes me to shake my head because it shows they lack integrity and good home training.

I could remember some years back, a young lady saw a young man driving an exotic car in the same street she lives with her parents; hastening, she quickly talked to the young man because she wants him to notice her, though the young man was a little bit matured than her: I thought he was going to shun her and move on with his life, but he gave in to her wiles and slept with her because he said; *'I didn't look for her, I am just helping her out to pass time and feel alright'.*The same way, many will do to other ladies and men to contact virus from one another because they are doing their wicked acts against each other. They were told not to commit fornication/adultery but no, they choose their own way because they love destruction and darkness, and easily give themselves to lust. Uncalled relationship dealt with Solomon, Samson, and Ahab.

# #16: PRIDE

This is an act that never take heed or correction but believes no one is more understanding, knowledgeable and superior than him/her at all things; for example, Lucifer and his agents. Isaiah 14:12-15 tells us of how the devil, Lucifer was cast out of Heaven because of lust and pride in his heart to enthrone himself as God, but he never succeeded, rather he was given shame as a reward to him and his cohorts that supported him: They were dethroned from their right and position. No one should allow pride overwhelm him/her because when you are asked to pray, you say for what am I not a Christian, the Lord has fought my battle on the Cross of Calvary and as soon as His blood touched the ground: He said, *"it is finished",* so every battle is finished and let me sleep in peace.

You don't know that even the devil was among the sons of God (Angels) when they came presenting themselves to God Almighty but they know not because he was wearing the same garment as everyone of them: God knew he was among them because He discerned him to be there amongst the true angels; and if not for God, that means Satan could deceive them. Pray when you are told to pray because your adversary is going to and fro looking for whom to devour and prayer is the key and Master's key to defeat to his onslaughts because that is the only thing the devil cannot do; but never call him a fool because he has been in this world before humans' existence. The act of pride can make you disobey because of too much familiarity with someone you are not supposed to get along with because you are too full of yourself.

Goliath with all his pride, where is he now? Yet, young David defeated him with a sling of stone; while he was with spear, sword and shield but God gave victory to David because he used the word God to shoot Goliath on the forehead, who had told David earlier in his pride saying *"I will feed you to the fowls of the air and beast of the field"*(1Samuel 17:44). The spirit of familiarity, which is pride brought Saul down from his throne and placed the young man, David on the throne because he was a man after God's heart, humble and obedient to God's instructions.

Pride made Nebuchadnezzar to leave his throne to eat grass in the bush like animals. Pride brought the downfall of Jezebel when she tried to lay hands on God's anointed called Elijah. She was thrown down from her quarter, despite that she was a queen and wild animals ate her up. Pride will make you lack manner of approach because you take people that are not your mate for granted and if time is not taken you might receive curse as reward. To those that look down on people because their parents are rich and they see others as nonentity and lazy, and refusing to make impact in others' lives are coming to face their pay-back because the Bible says, *"Give, it shall be given unto you, good measure, pressed down, shaken together and running over, so shall ye be given"*(Luke 6:38). When you do not have anything to give like money, let humility speak for you and through that act of humility in you, knowledge, understanding and wisdom will proceed from it because it is profitable and tender to life.

Pride made Adam to tell God that it is the woman, He gave to him that made him transgress against God and that word made him and his wife to be cast out of the Garden of Eden also called Paradise. Pride led Pharaoh into the Red-Sea because of his hardened heart and the words of his mouth which he said *"Who is the Lord, your God, for I know him not"* (Exodus 5:2). Pride brought the doom of Kohath, Dathan and Abiram, and their companions to doom because they were against Moses – the ground opened up and swallowed them. Pride will make many parents to regret that they gave birth to children because it will cost them so much embarrassment due to lack of home training and also the believe that they can talk rudely to people. The charm you so much trust will soon fail you one day, because nothing last forever, except God.

I heard what people were saying of a pastor, that he can walk on water like Lord Jesus, but immediately he stepped on the water, he drowned; another was saying he has broken the record of our Lord Jesus by fasting and praying for forty days and night, but he didn't last long and died. It is pride that can make someone to speak negatively about the gospel to say, *I don't need your Jesus, because I am more popular than Him, but was later found dead in her apartment'* because the name of the Lord is a strong tower, the righteous runs into it and he is save; His name should not be taken in vain or for granted because it has so much power and authority to set one free from captivity and to deliver. Pride can make you deaf and dumb to the truth; just like the message I read, a lady was going to party with her friends and the mother escorted her to where she was going to board a bus but her friends came with a truck filled with crate of eggs because the driver was taking their direction and the mother told her to commit the journey unto Jesus but she boldly said *'the truck is full except if Jesus can go sit where the crate of eggs are because there is no space in here for him':* After a while the mother received a call that her daughter had an accident with her friends and the truck driver; when the mother got there she found her daughter, friends and the driver dead, but when they checked the truck where the eggs are kept, there was no crack on them but were intact. That is to tell you that you should not take the name of the Lord in vain, no matter what. Pride brought Haman down and he was disgraced publicly because he was against the Jews, mostly Mordecai and the trap he set for Mordecai caught him; Haman fell into it and died.

Those that were against Daniel, and lied against him, were thrown into the lion's den and were consumed by lion. The reason is that they wanted to bring Daniel down and have their way to do more evil because of their selfishness and pride but they were put to shame for God was with Daniel. There are some I know to be too proud and they think irrationally, they imitate people and celebrities; they buy expensive phones, expensive clothes but starve themselves to impress people. Pride will make a man to say that according to our tradition, a woman should be in the kitchen; a woman should be seen and not heard. A woman cannot work but take care of her home and children but when expenses rise, you call her *'lazy woman, idiot, do you think money fall from tree, bed warming activities, baby making factory, and fool'* But you forgot that your pride did not allow you to look into the decision you made sometimes back; which makes man to beat his wife to prove that he is the man of the house.

Pride will make you see others opinion to be irrelevant because things should be done in your way and if they fail to do it your way, they will regret it and sometimes your plan may not matter or be relevant. Pride makes people say *'the church is meant for the poor not the rich', unknown to them that* everything they have or acquired are from God and His work. Thank goodness for His word that tells us what will befall those that talk like that and also put their trust in material things in the book of Ecclesiastes. Young boys and girls that don't know what life is all about call themselves big boys and girls and say they can handle things themselves, then they fall victim of what they cannot handle, and it is then they call on their parents to come and help them out: And because they are faster than their shadows and cannot learnt from the process of life gradually that life is not a bed of roses. Even the Bible says *"Jesus grew in wisdom, stature and favor with god and men"* (Luke 2:52). The ones with pride can lie and also try to force others to believe them because they cannot be corrected as if they know it all.

The opposite of Pride is Humility; there is someone that is not supposed to bring Himself low for us, that person is Jesus, He washed the feet of His disciples, He fasted and prayed for forty-days and nights, He prayed till His sweat became blood, He willingly gave His life for you and I to live and be reconciled back to God and God exalted Him by giving Him a name that is above all names; even demons tremble at the mention of the name of Jesus because it is filled with so much power and authority. Moses was humbled even unto death, many times did God tell him to allow Him to destroy the children of Israel and raise great and mighty nation from him but he pleaded on their behalf; he was called a meek man. David, a man after God's heart, was very humble because if he is told of his wrong doing, he admits immediately, he praised God; even when he was made king over Israel; even when God sent His servant, prophet Nathan to tell him that God has promised him that his children's children will rule His people forever, God also used His servant Prophet Nathan to tell him that his sins, He counts no more; he praised God more and more and always happy to hear them say *'Let us go into the house of God'.*

Job, a man God vouched for because right from when his mother gave birth to him, he never touched sin till he came of age even when Satan tried his best to kill his children, destroyed his livelihood; he never blamed God but exalted the name of the Lord. He helped the needy, but they laughed at him and mocked him; even his wife told him to curse God and die but he never listened to her. He humbled himself to God even his friends called him names and he rebuked them because he was accused of what he did not do.

# #17: WAY-OUT

1. **Surrender your life to Jesus:** Jesus is the way, the truth and the life; without Him, you can do nothing. Mind you, you have no power of your own but in Christ Jesus, in whom the Father, God is well pleased; you are an overcomer saved by His grace: Your salvation/prayer will not be hindered (Romans 12:1).

2. **Let God govern your life:** Let God take the wheel of your life, so the prince of this world (Satan) will not mislead you like the proverb of our Lord Jesus Christ about the sower, which is the word of God; some were glad to hear it and bear forth good fruits which is the soul they won to the Kingdom of God as Christ Jesus enabled them; some were also glad to hear it but their house was built on sand, that gave the devil access to deceive them from believing the truth, for they don't have a ***solid foundation*** in Christ Jesus, the Rock of Ages, the hope of the world: Some, their hearts were hardened to the word of God, no matter what one does to change them, they will never change. Mind you, God has given you free will to decide; He does not force one to serve Him (Psalm 37:5).

3. **Love your neighbor as yourself:** God is love, He loves us unconditionally, He is not a man that He should lie, He laid down His for us to live; if we claim to be Christians but hate one another, still we claim to be good, our worship to God is not true but false; for the Lord never hates anyone even on the Cross of Calvary, He said "*Father,*

*forgive them for they know not what they do"* that is true love, not false; pray for them that persecute you and if they change not, the Lord will heap ***coals of fire*** on them (Matthew 22:37-39).

4. **Be contented:** When you put your trust in God alone, not in mammon or the gods of this world, you will obey His word that says *"There is time for everything"* (Ecclesiastes 3:1-11).

5. **Let God lead you on the Path of Righteousness for His Name sake:** When the Lord is your shepherd; you will hearken and walk diligently to His word, for His sheep hear His voice and He is the Good Shepherd (Psalm 23).

6. **Reject every ungodly act, let God come into your life and make peace:** Blessed is he that walks not in ungodliness nor sit in the midst of the scornful, for the Lord your God is with you and prosper you (Psalm 1).

7. **Be of good courage for the Lord is ever ready to answer and bless you:** The Lord has not given us the Spirit of fear but of love, power, boldness and sound mind, as He was with Moses and He never failed him, He will be with you and never disappoint you (2 Timothy 1:7).

8. **Make God your Priority:** As a matter of fact, God should be our FIRST and LAST, we should walk with Him diligently; not familiar with Him as Judas Iscariot did and he perished. The Bible tells us of Enoch and how he walked with God from the beginning of his life till he was three hundred and

sixty five years old; and God took him neither did Enoch give excuses (Genesis 5:18-24).

9. **Always believe in the Name of the Lord:** The Name of the Lord is a ***strong tower***, His Name has so much power and authority that darkness cannot comprehend but tremble at the mention of His Name (Joel 2:32; Acts 2:21).

10. **Always look up to God, your Creator and Give of life during the time of peace and war:** Do not call on the Name of the Lord only when it is hard or you are attack; but also call on Him when all is well, so your adversary, the devil will not devour you: I believe the story of Job should shed light to it (Psalm

No matter the situation and circumstances you find yourself, never cease to praise the Lord, who gave you life and tolerates your sin: Let every living thing or organism praise the Lord, for He is God of the living, not of the dead (Psalm 150).

# CONCLUSION

It is better to appear stupid before men than to miss Heaven. Remain Blessed; and Rapturable

www.ingramcontent.com/pod-product-compliance
Lightning Source LLC
LaVergne TN
LVHW050326160826
845677LV00014B/3549

* 9 7 8 9 7 8 9 9 1 0 6 1 8 *